MY PRAYERS

By REV. JUDE WINKLER, OFM Conv.

Imprimi Potest: Daniel Pietrzak, OFM Conv., Minister Provincial of St. Anthony of Padua Province (USA)
Nihil Obstat: Francis McAree, S.T.D., Censor Librorum
Imprimatur: Patrick J. Sheridan, Vicar General, Archdiocese of New York

The Nihil Obstat and Imprimatur are official declarations that a book or pamphlet is free of doctrinal or moral error. No implication is contained therein that those who have granted the Nihil Obstat and Imprimatur agree with the contents, opinions or statements expressed.

CPSIA   August 2009   10 9 8 7 6 5 4 3 2 1   A/P

© 1990 by CATHOLIC BOOK PUBLISHING CORP., Totowa, N.J.
Printed in Hong Kong   ISBN 978-0-89942-490-3

Good Morning, God

When we wake up in the morning, we like to say good morning to all of the people whom we love. We say it to our parents, brothers, and sisters. We also say it to our friends when we go out to play or leave for school. Even if we are very tired, we try to wake up enough to give them a smile, because they are so important to us.

We should also say good morning to someone who is very, very important to us, to God. This way, right from the very start of our day, we will know that God is always with us. It also reminds us of how much we love Him and how much He loves us.

And so, the first thing in the morning, we call upon God. We begin our morning prayer with the sign of the cross, saying,

**In the name of the Father
and of the Son
and of the Holy Spirit.
Amen.**

Our Morning Prayer

We then begin to talk with God and to ask Him to bless our day. We can say anything that we want to Him because He is a very close friend and is always ready to listen to us.

One way that we might say our morning prayer is to pray something like this:

Good morning, God;
   thank You for this new day.

I will try to be good today
   and to help my mother and father
   and everyone else who needs my help.

Please be close to me all this day
   because I know that You are the Best Friend
   that anyone could ever have.

I love You, God.

The Prayer of St. Francis

Another way to say good morning to God is to say one of the prayers that have been said by good people for many, many years. One of these prayers is called the "Peace Prayer of St. Francis." In this prayer, we ask God to help us to be as good and as loving as He is.

Lord, make me an instrument of Your peace.
Where there is hatred, let me sow love;
where there is injury, pardon;
where there is doubt, faith;
where there is despair, hope;
where there is darkness, light;
and where there is sadness, joy.

Grant that I may not so much seek
to be consoled as to console;
to be understood, as to understand,
to be loved as to love.

For it is in giving that we receive;
it is in pardoning that we are pardoned,
and it is in dying that we are born to eternal life.

Asking for God's Help

While we are talking to God, we can also ask Him for all those things which we need as well as for the things that our family and friends need.

Some of the things we might pray for are:

If someone is sick —
   we pray that God might heal that person.
If someone is lonely —
   we pray that God might be close to that person.
If someone is poor —
   we pray that God might give that person food.
If someone has any type of problem —
   we pray that God might be with that person.

We also pray for people who are important to us:

We pray for our parents, grandparents, brothers, and sisters.
We pray for the Pope and bishops.
We pray for the President.
We pray for our teacher.

We can pray for people on their special days:

We pray for someone celebrating a birthday.
We pray for our parents on their anniversary.

God always listens to our prayers. He does not always give us the answer we wanted, but He will always give us whatever is best for us because He really loves us.

The Glory Be

Another way to pray is to praise God. We often do that with our family and friends. When someone gets a good hit while we are playing baseball and when someone does a good job in a play at school, we tell them that it was great. We tell the same thing to our Mom when she cooks a good meal and our Dad when he tells a funny story.

In the same way, we should tell God that we really respect Him and we think that He is wonderful. For many hundreds of years, the way that we have done that is to say a special prayer called the "Glory Be":

Glory be to the Father,
   and to the Son,
   and to the Holy Spirit.

As it was in the beginning
   is now
   and ever shall be.
Amen.

The Our Father

Another way that we show that God is special is to say the prayer called the "Our Father."

One day the disciples were listening to Jesus teach, and when He had finished they asked Him a favor. They had heard all sorts of prayers, and they wanted Jesus to teach them a special prayer that God would really like.

Jesus taught them that we should all call God our Father because He loves us as His very own children. He then taught the disciples and us to pray to God, our Father, as follows:

**Our Father,
Who art in heaven,
hallowed be Thy Name.
Thy kingdom come,
Thy will be done on earth as it is in heaven.**

**Give us this day our daily bread,
and forgive us our trespasses
as we forgive those who trespass against us.**

**And lead us not into temptation,
but deliver us from evil.**

The Hail Mary

God is not the only one whom we talk to in heaven. There are many people who were good and loving people while they were here on earth. When God called them home to heaven, they were so loving that they asked God if they could be both His friends and our friends until the end of time. We call these people "Saints."

The most special of the Saints is Mary, Jesus' own Mother. She was such a good and loving Mother that she not only held baby Jesus in her arms, but is also ready to hold each of us in her arms when we need her love.

The way we can call upon her is to say the prayer written for her:

Hail Mary, full of grace,
   the Lord is with you.

Blessed are you among women,
   and blessed is the fruit of your womb, Jesus.

Holy Mary, mother of God,
   pray for us sinners
   now and at the hour of our death,
Amen.

The Apostles' Creed

Another of the special prayers that we might want to learn is called the Apostles' Creed. This prayer teaches us all about God the Father, God the Son, and God the Holy Spirit. It is so special because we believe the very same things about God that the Apostles did, even though they lived over 2,000 years ago.

I believe in God, the Father almighty,
    creator of heaven and earth.

I believe in Jesus Christ, his only Son, our Lord.
    He was conceived by the power of the Holy Spirit
        and born of the Virgin Mary.
    He suffered under Pontius Pilate,
        was crucified, died, and was buried.
    He descended to the dead.
    On the third day he rose again.
    He ascended into heaven,
        and is seated at the right hand of the Father.
    He will come again to judge the living and the dead.

I believe in the Holy Spirit,
    the holy catholic Church,
    the communion of saints,
    the forgiveness of sins,
    the resurrection of the body,
    and the life everlasting. Amen.

How to Say the Rosary

Sometimes when we say our prayers, we say them all together to form one big prayer. One of these big prayers is called the "Rosary."

To say the Rosary, we begin with the Sign of the Cross. We then say the Apostles' Creed, three Hail Mary's, and a Glory Be.

After the Glory Be, we announce one of the mysteries of the Rosary. The mysteries are very important moments when God showed His love for all of us in a special way. We are supposed to think about that mystery while we pray first an Our Father and then ten Hail Mary's and a Glory Be.

When we have finished with these prayers, which we call a decade, we announce the next mystery and start a new decade of an Our Father, ten Hail Mary's and a Glory Be. There are five decades in all in our Rosary.

It is a good idea to hold a Rosary in our hand when we are praying it because otherwise we might lose track of how many of the prayers we have already said.

The Mysteries of the Rosary

The Joyful Mysteries

There are five mysteries which remember very happy moments during the lives of Jesus and Mary. These are called the Joyful Mysteries:

THE FIRST JOYFUL MYSTERY — The Annunciation
(When the Archangel Gabriel asked Mary to be the Mother of Jesus)

THE SECOND JOYFUL MYSTERY — The Visitation
(When Mary visited her cousin Elizabeth)

THE THIRD JOYFUL MYSTERY — The Birth of Jesus at Bethlehem

THE FOURTH JOYFUL MYSTERY — The Presentation of Baby Jesus in the Temple

THE FIFTH JOYFUL MYSTERY — The Finding of Jesus in the Temple

The Luminous Mysteries

Some of the mysteries remember very memorable moments in the lives of Jesus and Mary. These are called the Luminous Mysteries:

THE FIRST LUMINOUS MYSTERY — The Baptism of Jesus in the Jordan River

THE SECOND LUMINOUS MYSTERY — Christ's Self-Manifestation at the Wedding Feast of Cana

THE THIRD LUMINOUS MYSTERY — Christ's Proclamation of the Kingdom of God

THE FOURTH LUMINOUS MYSTERY — The Transfiguration of the Lord

THE FIFTH LUMINOUS MYSTERY — Christ's Institution of the Eucharist

The Sorrowful Mysteries

Some of the mysteries remember very sad moments in the lives of Jesus and Mary. These are called the Sorrowful Mysteries:

THE FIRST SORROWFUL MYSTERY — The Agony of Jesus in the Garden

THE SECOND SORROWFUL MYSTERY — The Scourging of Jesus at the Pillar

THE THIRD SORROWFUL MYSTERY — The Crowning of Jesus with Thorns

THE FOURTH SORROWFUL MYSTERY — The Carrying of the Cross by Jesus

THE FIFTH SORROWFUL MYSTERY — The Death of Jesus on the Cross

The Glorious Mysteries

Some of the mysteries remember very holy moments in the lives of Jesus and Mary. These are called the Glorious Mysteries:

THE FIRST GLORIOUS MYSTERY — The Resurrection of Jesus

THE SECOND GLORIOUS MYSTERY — The Ascension of Jesus into Heaven

THE THIRD GLORIOUS MYSTERY — The Descent of the Holy Spirit upon the Apostles

THE FOURTH GLORIOUS MYSTERY — The Assumption of Mary into Heaven

THE FIFTH GLORIOUS MYSTERY — The Crowning of Mary as Queen of Heaven and Earth

Asking God's Forgiveness

Sometimes we speak to God because we did something wrong and we want to ask His forgiveness. That is why we go to confession. We tell our sins to the priest, and he offers God's own forgiveness. Other times we ask God's forgiveness in our heart while we are at home or in school or wherever we are. We know that God will listen to us until we get a chance to go to confession.

One of the prayers we can use to ask God's forgiveness is the "Act of Contrition":

O my God,
    I am heartily sorry for having offended You,
    and I detest all my sins
    because of Your just punishments,
    but most of all because they have offended You,
        my God,
    Who are all good and deserving of all my love.

I firmly resolve
    with the help of Your grace
    to sin no more
    and to avoid the near occasions of sin.
Amen.

Prayers Before and After We Eat

Before we begin to eat, we should thank God for the food that we have in front of us and for the gift of our family. We should also pray for those who do not have enough to eat or those who do not have a family with whom they can eat.

One of the prayers we can say is:

Bless us, O Lord,
  and these, Your gifts,
    which we are about to receive from your goodness,
    through Christ our Lord.
Amen.

At the end of the meal we should thank God for the food that we have eaten and for being able to sit around our table with our family. We can say:

We give You thanks,
  Almighty God,
  for all Your gifts
    which we have received through Christ our Lord.
Amen.

Short Prayers During the Day

There are moments in every day when we can turn our thoughts to God and say short prayers that are especially composed for this purpose. They will remind us that God is always with us in everything we do.

Some of them are:

- **Thanks be to God.**
- **My God and my all.**
- **Lord, I love You.**
- **Praised be Jesus Christ.**
- **Heart of Jesus, I put my trust in You.**
- **My Jesus, mercy.**
- **Lord Jesus, bless all the children of the world.**
- **Holy Mary, pray for us.**

Examining Our Conscience

Now, after a long day, we are getting ready to go to bed. Before we fall asleep, though, there are two things that we should do. The first thing is that we should look back over all the things that we did that day and ask ourselves whether we did everything the way that we promised God we would do it. Some of the questions that we should ask ourselves are:

- Did we obey our parents?
- Did we always tell the truth?
- Did we try to help others?
- Did we say our prayers?
- Did we fight anyone?
- Did we make fun of anyone?
- Did we take anything that does not belong to us?
- Did we do our homework and our chores?

After we have finished asking ourselves these and other questions, we can ask God for forgiveness with an "Act of Contrition," page 23. We can also ask God's help to be better tomorrow.

Our Evening Prayer

Finally, before we go to sleep, we say good night to God, our friend.

One way that we can say good night is a short prayer:

Now I lay me down to sleep.
 I pray the Lord my soul to keep.
If I should die before I wake,
 I pray the Lord my soul to take.

But there are many other ways of saying good night to God. We might say something like:

Thank You, God,
 for being close to me all this day.

I am sorry if I was not always as good and kind as I should have been.

Help me to be a better person tomorrow.

Be by my side as I sleep tonight.

I love You, Jesus.

Good night.

Psalm 150

Praise the Lord!

Praise God in His glory!
Praise His power in heaven!
Praise Him for the mighty things
He has done!
Praise His wisdom and greatness!

Praise Him with trumpets and harps!
Praise Him with song and dancing!
Praise Him with bells and music!
Praise Him with joy and laughter!

Praise the Lord, all living creatures,
in heaven and on earth!

Praise the Lord!